YOUR KNOWLEDGE HAS VALUE

Bibliographic information published by the German National Library:

The German National Library lists this publication in the National Bibliography; detailed bibliographic data are available on the Internet at http://dnb.dnb.de .

Imprint:

Copyright © 2015 GRIN Verlag, Open Publishing GmbH
Print and binding: Books on Demand GmbH, Norderstedt Germany
ISBN: 978-3-668-00937-0

This book at GRIN:

http://www.grin.com/en/e-book/301540/critical-review-of-employees-perceptions-of-the-impact-of-work-on-health

Julia Steger

Critical Review of "Employees' perceptions of the impact of work on health behaviours" by N. Payne, F. Jones and P.R. Harris

GRIN Publishing

GRIN - Your knowledge has value

Since its foundation in 1998, GRIN has specialized in publishing academic texts by students, college teachers and other academics as e-book and printed book. The website www.grin.com is an ideal platform for presenting term papers, final papers, scientific essays, dissertations and specialist books.

Critical Review of *Employees' perceptions of the impact of work on health behaviours* by Payne, N, Jones, F., & Harris, P.R. (2012)

Julia Steger

Abstract: This paper gives a critical appraisal of the work of Payne et al. It shows that the sample and study design are limited by different sampling errors like selection bias or participant effects. The study results are acknowledged and brought into context. Finally the paper gives recommendations of how the study could have been improved.

Keywords: critical appraisal ◆ health behaviours ◆ work

Payne, N., Jones, F., & Harris, P. R. (2013). Employees' perceptions of the impact of work on health behaviours. Journal of health psychology, 18(7), 887-899.

Introduction

This paper will analyse the strengths and limitations of Peyne (Middlesex University, UK), Jones (University of Leeds, UK) and Harris' (University of Sheffield, UK; 2013) qualitative study on the employees' perceptions of the impact of work on health behaviours. The argument is going to be developed through a critical review of the journal article, focusing on the methodology used and its impact on the relevance of the results.

Payne at al. conducted semi-structured interviews with twenty-four employees of the UK site of a multinational company acting in the computer hardware and software industry (main areas of work: design, marketing and sales). The researchers obtained information about the employee's understanding of four defined health behaviours (namely smoking, drinking alcohol, exercise and diet) and how they are affected by their work. They identified four categories as the main themes affecting health behaviours, which are *work environment*, *business events*, *being busy at work* and *work stress* with various sub-categories.

As there already is a broad range of both qualitative and quantitative research relating to work and health, which is a circumstance the authors are aware of, they list a number of reasons to justify the study. They point out that the study is able to provide a complete picture of the topic by the range of factors and key behaviours it observes, the bottom-up approach as well as looking at both positive and negative impacts of work.

Payne, Jones and Harris conclude, that their study shows how work appeared to both constrain and promote healthy behaviour for different persons in different situations. They add, that employees are aware they sometimes only use work stress as an excuse for unhealthy behaviour and it's not necessarily the main or only reason for it.

Importance of the topic

First of all, the main strength of the paper, the high importance of the topic, must be highlighted and has to be described further. As the authors explain, work has a very important impact on different health behaviours, like smoking, alcohol consumption, a healthy diet and exercise, and therefore people's overall health. With cardiovascular diseases being the dominating causes of death in the modern world (Kelly & Fuster, 2010), which can be influenced by a more healthy lifestyle, this is a serious and important topic that needs further

intensive research. Although the topic of work's influence on health is broadly researched, there is indeed little qualitative study, what backs the need for this certain research up. It is interesting that Payne et al. use the bottom-up approach and it should help them and the readers identify what all the topics really affecting employee's behaviours are.

Most studies manly focus on *works stress* (Cox, Kuk, & Leiter, 1993; Ganster, 1991; Nelson & Simmons, 2003; Ng & Jeffery, 2003; Quick, Murphy, & Hurrell Jr., n.d.), whereas this paper identified three other different occupation related themes that affect health behaviours. They, too, consider four different behaviours and do not concentrate on a single one.

Therefore the results of the study – the four categories of work's impact on employees - should give a good starting point for further research and thus implications for improving those behaviours.

The authors describe and explain the existing research, both qualitative and quantitative, and the importance of the study in the first two parts of their paper (Payne, Jones, & Harris, 2013, pp. 887–889).

Sample and Method

However, the relevance of the results might not be as high as proposed by the authors due to a number of concerns, which are discussed hereafter.[1]

The first thing to consider is the sample. Its size of twenty-four participants seems relatively small at first. However, considering the method (qualitative study, semi-structured interviews) and resources like time or access and comparing the size to other qualitative studies (Mason, 2010), the sample size might be subordinate and acceptable in this case, but still has room for improvement. A big problem of this sample size and the way of presenting the results (quotes with age and gender of the participant) is, that it is easily possible to identify individuals, especially for other managers and employees of the company, like line managers or colleagues. This lack of anonymity is very likely to affect the participants' answers, as they won't be speaking as freely as if being unknown. They might have reservations to speak completely truthful because they don't want to be believed lazy or in any level addicted to alcohol. There is another source that influences employees' replies, which will be discussed later. Even more important than the size is the quality and representativeness of the sample. From this point of view, it lacks a lot of substance: all employees are working in the same

---

[1] Although the concept of 'reliability and validly' is not accepted by some qualitative researchers, both measurements are going to be addressed in this paper. This is, because the framework can partly be applied to the qualitative study and is helpful to evaluate how sound the work is. Some evaluation will be based on Guba's and Lincoln's framework on how reliability and validity can be applied to qualitative research (1985).

firm, country and sector and at that same company site. All are white-collar workers wherefore a certain higher education or academic degree is presumed. The participants differ from each other only in their internal variety, which, for itself, is rather diverse, including a random range of gender, age, specific job and the hierarchy level they inherent. The fact that the group of participants is so very specific affects the reliability of the study, as a different, more random choice is very likely to give different results. The behaviours described in the study are highly influenced by the company's culture. Thus, other companies with other values in their culture might have another effect on their employees. And those vary even more between different sectors and industries, where employees may live completely different lifestyles. This makes it extremely difficult to generalise the given results.

The problem described above can be defined as a sampling error, as the sample does not represent the wider population. Additionally, the participants were not randomly selected within the company but they volunteered themselves. This is another facet of the sampling error, the (self-)selection bias. Payne et al. address especially this issue in the limitations section of their article, next to listing the already mentioned sampling error (2012, p.897). They describe that employees who are willing to participate might be more interested in health behaviours than their peers or in sparing the time for the interview. A more random sample of the same size wherefore the participation is mandatory might therefore give more general results and might probably show a different level of awareness or interest in health behaviours.

Because of all the above, the sample is very specific and the means of data generation could be seen as not very reliable. The authors, however, argue that the purpose of a qualitative study is not to be universal or general. Although a more random and reliable sample would have been desirable, there are reasons, why the overall themes and sub-themes are reliable, which will be described later on.

The mere quality and reliability of the instruments of conducting and recording the interviews appear to be reliable and adequate in terms of the methods and procedures used. The content of the interview is not quoted exactly but clearly described, and appropriate recording and transcription tools were used. The semi-structured interview has in this case the most advantages over structured or unstructured interviews. It helps to cluster answers and covers all areas of researchers' interest by starting with and including certain standard questions and topics to cover without constraining the interviewee. Thus, it leaves room for employees' thoughts, which the researchers haven't thought of during the design of the interview or helps

the interviewer to tailor the question to the flow of conversation. Finally, the use of open-ended questions fits the authors' bottom-up approach and openness towards new thoughts.

Another rather general issue of the method is its vulnerability for response biases. As already described above, due to the fact that the interviews are conducted face-to-face and cannot be considered anonymous because of the small sample and detailed referencing of the quotes, the participants might not be completely truthful with their answers. Payne, Jones and Harris refer to this in the limitations section, describing that the employees might try to satisfy what they perceive to be expectations of the researcher or society. This is a big concern about that method, as it is likely, that people will not answer or speak completely freely or honestly about some topics, e.g. concerning questions regarding above-average alcohol consumption. However, it would be very costly and time consuming to use more accurate, objective methods (Strecher, Becker, Clark, & Prasada-Rao, 1989). A way to improve this will be described later.

Consequently, here must be some doubts regarding the validity, as well. The data presents the views and perceptions of a certain group of people within this company. However, it might not accurately represent the social concept the authors want to examine in general, that is how employees perceive the effects of work on their health behaviours, due to its specific sample. Secondly, as concerning external validity, Payne, Jones and Harris explain in their conclusion (2013, p. 897) that work may only be one aspect affecting health behaviour. They acknowledge that employees often use work only as an excuse to devote themselves to unhealthy practices. The study results are therefore only a very specific part of different impacts on health behaviour that might correlate and interrelate with each other. Future research needs to take this into consideration.

Analysis and Results

Due to the mentioned concerns, the confidence to discuss the reported results is negatively affected at first. In comparison to their method of choosing a sample and conducting the interviews, however, the analysis seems to be sound. Payne, Jones and Harris used a method of evaluating their data with a thematic analysis based on Braun and Clarke (2006), whose model is widely used and referenced. The six step process is described and explained in the 'analysis' section of the paper. It includes intensive examination of the data, assigning the answers to categories, grouping them into themes, reviewing those themes in relation to the

data as a whole, naming the specific categories and finally producing the report with supporting quotes. The authors used an independent researcher to achieve interrater reliability, which is an important tool to ensure constancy and corroboration, and thus confirmability (Lincoln & Guba, 1985). The result was with .70 a "acceptable" (Payne et al., 2013, p. 890) degree of agreeableness.

The outcomes of the thematic analysis are the following themes and sub-themes: "the *work environment*, including policy, convenience and workplace cultural norms; *business events* effecting one's routine and again convenience and workplace cultural norms; *being busy at work* effecting time and energy for healthy behaviour; and *work stress* leading to health behaviours being used as coping responses on bad and good days" (Payne et al., 2013, p. 887).

Payne et al. amplify the details of the findings thereafter. The themes and sub-themes are described in detail, positive and negative dimensions and examples are added and substantiated with quotes. After that, the authors discuss how the four health behaviours are affected by the work impacts and they define and link these assumptions to existing research.

Summing the discussion up, work influences health behaviours both positive and negative, however unfavourable influences are more likely to occur. In some cases both negative and positive occurrences helped some people to increase healthy behaviour (e.g. going to the gym), but fostered adverse reaction in others (e.g. drinking alcohol). For still others, those influences correlated even more diverse. Nonetheless, work shows to be a rather negative impact on healthy behaviours in general.

Due to the method used, the study can't describe the underlying reasons for the behaviours. It only shows the employees' own perception, which could differ from the actual impacts. The authors address to this issue and explain, that this is a result of the specific and individual-oriented aim on focusing on the participants understanding.

Qualification of the Critique

Due to the qualitative nature of the study some of the listed issues must now be qualified more detailed. Although the study might lack reliability and validly, other criteria needs to be taken into consideration, as well. Qualitative data is not easily transferable in general, as only small and specific, but very detailed samples are used. The authors did describe the method of the study and the questions and content of the interview well enough to allow other researchers to use or replicate it, but these must use their own judgement to define if a transfer will be sensible or not.

Secondly, themes were confirmed by an independent rater, the results were compared to external influences and the authors addressed most limitations within their paper.

Thus, it can finally be assumed, that the overall themes and sub-themes are relevant and acceptable. Maybe their described extend and dimensions are too specific for a general model, but in their overarching purpose the categories seem to be useful. To ensure the validity and significance of the results (especially the themes and sub-themes), a few recommendations should be taken into consideration.

Recommendations

The authors could improve their results by implementing a quantitative follow-up study to verify those themes and to get more information about the importance of the various dimensions. All the themes or items should be analysed, for example by using factor analysis. First, a confirmatory factor analysis would be suggestive to ensure that the themes match the researchers' hypothesis. Afterwards, the (potentially) corrected facets can be tested with various models and when the themes are academically proven to be valid and reliable, a large and anonymous survey can be used to show a general image of how work influences health behaviours. From there on, it will be more easy to make suggestions than it is now, as the given answers concerning the different behaviours varied a lot between the participants in this study.

Apart from that, there are some recommendations that could be made to develop the present study itself. First and most important would be the improvement of the sample: the size is definitely one point to bear in mind and reconsider to extend, but a more random sample would be even more vital and necessary. The results and their significance can be enhanced significantly by interviewing a wider range of employees from different companies and different sectors. It is questionable if and why Payne, Jones and Harris were so limited in their participants.

Secondly, to ensure the anonymity of the participants, some precarious information could have been attained using a different style of questioning. As those topics can be very intimate for some people, the authors could have used online or hard copy questionnaires to directly address sensitive topics like alcohol consumption as this leaves the employees identity unknown. However, it must be taken into consideration that parts of the interviews are no longer connected then, which might pose a problem for the researchers.

Conclusion

In conclusion, Payne, Jones and Harris attempted to define the important themes that occur in the workplace and affect employees' health behaviours. Although the methods are not entirely sound and show a lot of room for improvement, the themes might still be applicable. To ensure that, however, future research, especially quantitative studies, is necessary. Other aspects to be considered by future research could be the focus on underlying influences and the utilisation of the results to develop interventions and development areas for companies to improve their employees' health.

References:

Braun, V., & Clarke, V. (2006). Using thematic analysis in psychology. *Qualitative Research in Psychology*. Retrieved from http://www.tandfonline.com/doi/abs/10.1191/1478088706qp063oa

Cox, T., Kuk, G., & Leiter, M. (1993). Burnout, health, work stress, and organizational healthiness.

Ganster, D. C. (1991). Work Stress and Employee Health. *Journal of Management, 17*(2), 235–271. doi:10.1177/014920639101700202

Kelly, B., & Fuster, V. (2010). Promoting Cardiovascular Health in the Developing World:: A Critical Challenge to Achieve Global Health. Retrieved from http://books.google.co.uk/books?hl=de&lr=&id=hjdkAgAAQBAJ&oi=fnd&pg=PP1&d q=Promoting+Cardiovascular+Health+in+the+Developing+World:+A+Critical+Challen ge+to+Achieve+Global+Health&ots=Fc7yshGHGr&sig=_jpJtwmdw0CFtGnL1qaK-k-8Iig

Lincoln, Y. S., & Guba, E. G. (1985). *Naturalistic Inquiry* (p. 416). Newbury Park, CA: SAGE Publications. Retrieved from http://books.google.com/books?hl=en&lr=&id=2oA9aWlNeooC&pgis=1

Mason, M. (2010, August 24). Sample Size and Saturation in PhD Studies Using Qualitative Interviews. *Forum Qualitative Sozialforschung / Forum: Qualitative Social Research*. Retrieved from http://www.qualitative-research.net/index.php/fqs/article/view/1428/3027

Nelson, D., & Simmons, B. L. (2003). Health psychology and work stress: A more positive approach. In J. Campbell & L. E. Tetrick (Eds.), *Handbook of occupational health psychology* (pp. 97–119). Washington, DC, US: American Psychological Association.

Ng, D. M., & Jeffery, R. W. (2003). Relationships between perceived stress and health behaviors in a sample of working adults. *Health Psychology : Official Journal of the Division of Health Psychology, American Psychological Association, 22*(6), 638–42. doi:10.1037/0278-6133.22.6.638

Payne, N., Jones, F., & Harris, P. R. (2013). Employees' perceptions of the impact of work on health behaviours. *Journal of Health Psychology, 18*(7), 887–99. doi:10.1177/1359105312446772

Quick, J. C., Murphy, L. R., & Hurrell Jr., J. J. (n.d.). *Stress & well-being at work: Assessments and interventions for occupational mental health.*

Strecher, V. J., Becker, M. H., Clark, N. M., & Prasada-Rao, P. (1989). Using patients' descriptions of alcohol consumption, diet, medication compliance, and cigarette smoking. *Journal of General Internal Medicine, 4*(2), 160–166. doi:10.1007/BF02602359

YOUR KNOWLEDGE HAS VALUE

Bibliographic information published by the German National Library:

The German National Library lists this publication in the National Bibliography; detailed bibliographic data are available on the Internet at http://dnb.dnb.de .

Imprint:

Copyright © 2015 GRIN Verlag, Open Publishing GmbH
Print and binding: Books on Demand GmbH, Norderstedt Germany
ISBN: 9783668230743

This book at GRIN:

http://www.grin.com/en/e-book/323340/the-central-banks-of-europe-japan-the-u-s-and-the-u-k-their-policy

William Garner

The Central Banks of Europe, Japan, the U.S. and the U.K. Their Policy Responses to Specific Sets of Economic Challenges

GRIN Publishing

GRIN - Your knowledge has value

Since its foundation in 1998, GRIN has specialized in publishing academic texts by students, college teachers and other academics as e-book and printed book. The website www.grin.com is an ideal platform for presenting term papers, final papers, scientific essays, dissertations and specialist books.

Visit us on the internet:

http://www.grin.com/

http://www.facebook.com/grincom

http://www.twitter.com/grin_com

Critically Evaluate Whether The Central Banks of Europe, Japan, The U.S. and The U.K. Have Been Taking The Appropriate Policy Responses To Their Specific Set of Economic Challenges.

Firstly it is important to define what the economic challenges are to understand and explain how the policies are used to achieve these. Economic challenges are usually associated with a countries economic objectives which generally include sustainable economic growth, low targeted inflation and also the more argued topic of full employment. According to Vickery (1993) full employment is: "a situation where there are at least as many job openings as there are persons seeking employment, probably calling for a rate of unemployment, as currently measured, of between 1 and 2 percent". This partially agrees but argues with Beveridge's well known definition argued that there will always be unemployment due to frictional unemployment so argued that 'full employment' exists when there is around 3% unemployment. There are other objectives such as public finances, inequality and environmental issues, although the three main objectives tend to take priority and precedence to other objectives especially when evaluating the role of central banks and the economy. In terms of central banks for these nations, they are all in control of monetary policy, so it needs to be analysed how effective monetary policy is to respond to economic challenges. Before analysing the role of the central banks, Europe, is a Union of countries and thereby needs to be quantifiably subjected compared to the individual nations of Japan, the U.S. and the U.K. The European Central Bank will represent Europe and its 19 EU member states that use the Euro currency, this will help put into perspective the policy of the European Central Bank (ECB).

The European Central Bank has control over monetary policy of its 19 EU member states that use the Euro currency and are thereby required to manage the stability of the Euro and inflation and also to assist in controlling the European Economy. In order to achieve their economic objectives, the ECB has only a 'one size fits all' scenario in that they have to adapt monetary policy over all these countries. Issing (2014) argues that "The ECB therefore focuses on its own mandate, with the primary objective to maintain price stability, leaving others to meet their own responsibilities." He goes on to say that: "One size *must* fit all". This approach of the ECB allows independence of monetary policy from political involvement while governments in the Eurozone can take care of their own fiscal policy and not influence the short-term of an economy for political gains .In the case of the ECB, fiscal policy is down to its member states to manage themselves as the ECB has no involvement in taxation and government spending. This is arguably not the best for certain countries, Nedvěd states that: "…Ireland, Greece and Spain experienced relatively high

inflation rates and highly positive output gaps...they needed to raise the interest rates. Nevertheless, they were not able to do that since the monetary policy had been in hands of the ECB and the interest rates had been tailored to the whole Eurozone." This argument emphasises the difficulties in managing multiple economies through monetary policy as it can't be used to control the economies of certain countries whose economies aren't in line with other members of the Euro.

The global financial crisis that hit in 2007 led to high unemployment in many of the countries in the Eurozone. Eurostat states that in August 2014 Greece had an unemployment level of 25.9% while Spain had 24.2% unemployed. This unemployment level is very large and has not only damaged economic growth and political parties but also caused poverty and other issues such as stagflation. To counter this, the ECB has decided to buy bundles of asset-backed securities (ABS) and covered bonds, in mind to increase the price level closer to its target of 2% and hopefully increase confidence within the EU in terms of banks lending more to businesses and consumers. Jones (2014) states that "By signaling the ECB's intent to rid the currency area of the very real threat of economic stagnation, a sizeable, broad programme of private-sector asset purchases could damp pessimism. As the same time, it is likely to weaken the euro, aiding the region's exporters..." This benefits the EU as exports brings cash flows into the EU and increases economic growth potentially while also leading to investment from businesses in expanding and trading abroad. Jens Weidmann, President of the Deutsche Bundesbank (2014), however, disagrees with the ECB and what Jones has to say, stating in a speech that: "The biggest bottleneck for growth in the euro area is not monetary policy, nor is it the lack of fiscal stimulus: it is the structural barriers that impede competition, innovation and productivity." This might signal that more cohesion between the ECB and policy makers in that there may be too much 'bureaucracy' and 'red tap' and not enough of a 'free market' system within Europe for businesses to grow and compete allowing for more employment, economic growth and an increase in the price level. In the case of the ECB, they are trying to do all they can to spark the EU Economy with what they have and have made some progress through setting measures on financial institutions to try and prevent another banking crisis, however, it might be up to policy makers in the EU to allow for less of a bureaucratic system and to not 'crowd out' businesses.

The Bank of Japan has similar functions which the Bank's charter states that the three functions of the BOJ is to be: "Issuer of banknotes", "Bank of banks" and the "Bank of the government", while also being in charge of monetary policy, independent of the government's political agenda. Japan has struggled with periods of stagnation pushed by the lowering of average wages. Etsuro Honda, an advisor to Prime Minister Shinzō *Abe*

and key to Abe's reflationary policies states in an interview with Reuters that: "In order for income effects to work, wages must increase". One of the methods of re-inflating the economy is through quantitative easing. An article by the Economist (31/10/2014) states that the new expansion on quantitative easing will "swell Japan's monetary base at an even faster pace, by around ¥80 trillion ($712 billion) each year". The result of this is not only does it increase inflation due to more currency being injected into the economy but investor's may expect further inflation so in the case of Japan which required inflation will raise confidence and expectations for growth. On top of this it may also lead to more bonds being sold while lower interest rates will encourage businesses to grow through investing by borrowing at low rates. Consumers may also get cheap credit for purchases, this should theoretically allow Japan to grow. According to the theory on aggregate demand, an increase in consumption (C) and investment (I) in the formula of AD = C+I+G+(X-M). Figure 1.1 (RevisionGuru 2015) indicates the impact on aggregate demand of an increase in consumption and investment if everything else is equal will cause the aggregate demand to shift to the right from (AD) to (AD1). The impact of this is the price level increases from (P) to (P1) and the national income/output to increase from (Y) to (Y1), while the equilibrium rises from (P) (Y) to (P1) (Y1) upwards along the aggregate supply curve. This method appeals to Japan as it should help to try and push up wages, employment and the price level in the economy benefiting growth in the short-run aggregate supply. Keynes argued that: "Long run is a misleading guide to current affairs. In the long run we are all dead." As mentioned, this may seem all fine in theory, however, aggregate demand theory is considered highly short term and may not be beneficial in the long-term as confidence of say quantitative easing may disappear if the scheme isn't that successful. McLannahan (2014) states at the end of the year that: "a variety of indicators suggest that broad inflation expectations are flat, if not falling. The BoJ's own quarterly survey showed that companies' forecasts of rises in output prices were weaker in December than in October, almost across the board." McLannahan goes on to state that "A preliminary CPI reading for December in the Tokyo area – considered a leading indicator for the rest of the country – showed core inflation at just 0.3 per cent, excluding tax effect." This result is extremely damaging for Abe and his "Abenomics" reflationary plans whose inflationary target of 2 per cent is not being met. This is only made worse with the chief strategist at SMBC Friend Securities in Tokyo, Toshihiko Matsuno (2014) stating that: "Many investors do not believe that Japan can get pulled out of deflation." This notions that the Bank of Japan is struggling to inflate the economy, however, there are other methods that could help them to do this. Pesek states that "liquidity isn't enough; banks and corporations need incentive to tap that money." This is one of the main issues of quantitative easing in that, if the money isn't being spread and injected into the

3

economy to businesses and consumers, inflation may not be as strong. One of the major recent issues that is also not helping the Japanese economy in inflating is the drop in the price of oil. According to the CNBC oilprice (2014), crude oil on the 6th January oil prices closed on $48.46 a huge drop from 6th October to $87.67 on close. Japan imports a majority of its oil which in terms could be considered good as there would be lower fuel prices for consumers and lower the current account deficit, however, this may not necessarily inflate prices as energy prices would also decrease for energy providers in Japan meaning it would impact the effort to raise inflation.

Japan's central bank could have done more to turn around the economy and alternatives to just quantitative easing. Pesek discusses on a Bloomberg report that the BOJ could "consider buying up the nation's most distressed properties and egregious white-elephant projects….Buying the "zaito bonds" state-run companies issue to fund projects, a range of asset-backed and mortgage-backed securities…" The impact of this would be to inject the money created from quantitative easing to inflate the economy for example by pumping money into the housing market which should allow the economy to grow through the multiplier effect. This should hopefully increase employment and consumption within the economy and allow it to grow which in turn increase confidence for investment from businesses and also in the form of foreign direct investment (FDI). Callen et al. argue slightly differently from Pesek addressing that "both corporate and banking sector weaknesses share the blame for the decline in bank credit." Because of the issue in the regulations and management of the banking sector there is not enough borrowing and thereby less spending in the economy which causes a dampening of the inflationary measures. According to the nationaldebtclocks (2014) website, the national debt of Japan totals 198.59% of GDP which is the highest on the planet and therefore is almost a necessity for the central bank to try and stimulate the economy to grow with monetary policy while the government can use fiscal policy alongside this. If the central bank focused more on these issues discussed by Pesek and Callen et al. rather than focusing significantly on quantitative easing, the BOJ could increase the price level and also confidence in the Japanese economy which would allow large investment flows into the economy and allow Japan to try and address its debt crisis.

The United States Federal Reserve is also in charge of monetary policy although its objectives are varied compared to many other central banks. Its key methods involve monetary policy and regulation of the banking industry, however, according to the Federal Reserve Act of 1913 Section 2A: "…promote effectively the goals of maximum employment, stable prices, and moderate long-term interest rates." This policy is often referred to as the "dual mandate" which Thomas defines as: "mandate given to the central

bank to maintain both price level stability and maximum sustainable employment." Unlike other central banks, the Federal Reserve also has to cater its monetary policy in line with 'maximum sustainable employment' which can arguably be a trade-off when also trying to maintain a stable price level. Figure 1.2 shows 'The Phillips Curve', this illustrates the trade-off between inflation and the rate of unemployment. When monetary decisions such as lowering interest rates can cause more spending in the economy due to ease of borrowing leading to an increase in consumption causing aggregate demand to increase leading to growth. One of the impacts of this is a potential increase in the price level. In the case of the diagram, if this happened while the rate of inflation is at (P2), while the rate of unemployment is at (N2) causing the equilibrium to be at (b). The inflation from the lower interest rates could cause the price level to rise to (p1), this will readjust the equilibrium to point (a) causing the rate of unemployment to decrease to (N1). This inverse relationship between both the rate of inflation and unemployment means that the Federal Reserve is likely to have problems when using monetary policy to try and maintain a stable inflationary and unemployment rate.

One of the major issues the U.S. has is their trade deficit. The trade deficit as indicated by Figure 1.3 shows that in the last ten year, the United States has been dealing with a trade deficit in goods and services showing that the US has been importing more than exporting. This essentially means that in relation to the circular flow of income that there are more withdrawals of liquidity leaving the country that coming into it. This can reduce confidence in the economy and also aggregate demand meaning that economic growth may not be as high as possible. The Federal Reserve may not be doing enough to try and improve the balance of payments deficit as it has quite steady in the last four years between $30,000 million and $50,000 million as shown by Figure 1.3. The exchange rate of the US currency may be partly the problem, due to imports from countries such as China and India where costs of production are significantly lower meaning it is cheaper to import from those countries particularly when the US dollar is strong in terms of the exchange rate. The Federal Funds Rate has been set at 0.25% over the last 4 years, this is likely to lead to less attractiveness of foreign direct investment due to a lack of confidence in the economy as a higher stable interest rate is often common in a strong economy. Alternatively, trying to lower the value of the dollar would make U.S. exports more competitive in overseas market while also hopefully lower imports as local products would also be more competitive with imports. They could lower the value of the dollar by devaluing the currency such as adding more US dollars into the foreign exchange market although there could be other economic complications of doing this. However, the Federal Reserve may arguably be responding correctly to the balance of payments. Kuepper states that: "the U.S. may have a large trade deficit, but since most of its goods and

services are produced and consumed domestically, this trade deficit doesn't have a major impact on its overall GDP." The trade deficit, although large is reasonably stable while US exports may increase to large markets such as China where there has been somewhat liberalisation of markets. The US currency is also relatively stable indicating confidence which should allow for foreign direct investment without having to devalue while the size of the US economy does not necessarily mean the balance of payments needs to be sorted, however, not as drastically as perhaps the countries debt.

The Bank of England's (BOE) monetary policy objectives according to the BOE is to "deliver price stability – low inflation – and, subject to that, to support the Government's economic objectives including those for growth and employment." These objectives are similar to the United States Federal Reserve although the BOE focuses majorly on inflation over other objectives in trying to meet the 2% target. Barty argues that the BOE should be focusing more on other objectives over inflation stating: "...there has been excessive focus on inflation targeting under Sir Mervyn King at the expense of financial stability and growth." He goes on to state that: "We suggested that the new Governor be given a mandate to support growth, in particular to ensure that credit once again starts flowing...nominal GDP targeting has raised the issue of whether this might be a way to change the Bank's mandate." Under the new governor Mark Carney, ideas such as using nominal GDP that takes into account inflation could potentially be used as the Bank's mandate that would take into account inflation and also a spotlight on growth.

One of the major challenges is the reforming of the financial system that caused the 2008 recession and the economic shocks it caused globally. Mark Carney, stated in speech that: "Banks are now much more resilient. They have more capital, more liquidity and are less susceptible to procyclical spirals." He continues to say that: "The foundations are laid. The next stage of reform should build a system that serves households and businesses to its full potential." Wolf argues against this stating "Unfortunately, policymakers failed to sustain the policies required to support private-sector de-leveraging and so avoid a prolonged balance-sheet recession. Largely as a result, the recovery proved weak or even withered away altogether in 2011 and 2012." Both Carney and Wolf argue differently although are both partly right, there has been some reforms although perhaps not enough which has left many private-sector businesses without an ability to gain loans in struggling times. Although there has been a solid basis for reforms, it can be agreed that the Eurozone crisis has hindered the recovery.

The recession took a toll on unemployment levels of up to 8.4% in October 2011, however since then this has dropped to 5.9% in August 2014 according to Eurostat. This could be down to recent growth in the economy of 2.6% GDP growth in 2014. The reason behind

economic growth is partially down to low stable interest rates encouraging borrowing and investment which in turn increases revenue for businesses and higher employment through the 'multiplier effect'. The bank focus on low interest rates has helped stimulate the economy and in term increase employment, economic growth without a trade-off of high inflation which is currently very low partially due to the plummet in the price of oil. The BOE have managed to meet its objectives and challenges although can continue to grow on accomplishments in financial reforms and continuing to stimulate strong economic growth and decreasing unemployment.

The weight of the evidence indicates that the recession that hit in 2008 caused huge economic shocks around the globe. Governments such as the United States, the United Kingdom, Japan and those in Europe have spent huge numbers in bailing out banks and funding large fiscal policy plans to help recover economies, not to mention bailing out countries such as the EU bailing out Greece. All three of these nations and many of those in the EU are all developed nations who are struggling with a current account deficits due to developing countries and other countries with low cost factors of production. The central banks have done a lot such as adjusting interest rates to increase confidence to try and spark lending, although without proper reforms of the banking sector there could be further issues. The Bank of Japan may not be dealing with its budget deficit sufficiently hence why low interest rates aren't pushing growth in the economy as less confidence due to the deficit so less investment, on top of this liquidity from quantitative easing isn't necessarily going to consumers. Another issue is the trade deficit meaning difficulties in obtaining steady economic growth. The United States and the United Kingdom have similar issues although are starting to see economic growth but still need to deal with debt, large budget and current account deficits. In terms of dealing with challenges, the central banks have responded reasonably well to the economic challenges although the fact that central banks only have control over monetary policy cannot solve all problems due to trade-offs. In order to manage economic issues, a mixture of monetary and fiscal policy is needed along with a variety of reforms, this is because budget deficits and large amounts of debt can have an effect on confidence and investment.

Bibliography

Bankofengland.co.uk, (2015). *Monetary Policy Framework*. [online] Available at: http://www.bankofengland.co.uk/monetarypolicy/Pages/framework/framework.aspx [Accessed 23 Jan. 2015].

Barty, J. (2013). *Should the Bank of England's objective be changed?* [online] Policy Exchange. Available at: http://www.policyexchange.org.uk/media-centre/blogs/ category/item/should-the-bank-of-england-s-objective-be-changed [Accessed 23 Jan. 2015].

Callen, T. and Ostry, J. (2015). *Japan's Lost Decade. Policies for Economic Revival*. Washington D.C.: International Monetary Fund, p.45.

Carney, M. (2014). *The Future of Financial Reform*.

Chicagofed.org, (2015). *The Federal Reserve's Dual Mandate - Federal Reserve Bank of Chicago*. [online] Available at: https://www.chicagofed.org/publications/speeches/our-dual-mandate [Accessed 17 Jan. 2015].

European Central Bank; Otmar Issing, (2005). *One size fits all! A single monetary policy for the euro area*. [Speech] Available at: http://www.ecb.europa.eu/press/key/date/ 2005/html/sp050520.en.html [Accessed 28 Dec. 2015].

Federalreserve.gov, (2013). *FRB: Federal Reserve Act: Section 2a*. [online] Available at: http://www.federalreserve.gov/aboutthefed/section2a.htm [Accessed 17 Jan. 2015].

Jones, C. (2014). *ECB preview " Three key ABS challenges*. [online] Financial Times. Available at: http://blogs.ft.com/the-world/2014/10/qa-the-ecbs-asset-buying-plan/ [Accessed 13 Jan. 2015].

Krugman, P. (2010). *In The Long Run, We Are Still All Dead*. [online] Paul Krugman Blog. Available at: http://krugman.blogs.nytimes.com/2010/06/25/in-the-long-run-we-are-still-all-dead/ [Accessed 28 Dec. 2014].

McLannahan, B. (2014). Japan inflation slips to 14-month low. *Financial Times*.

Oilprice.com, (2015). *Oil Prices & Energy News: Crude Oil Price Charts, Investment Advice*. [online] Available at: http://oilprice.com/commodity-price-charts?1&page= chart&sym=CLH15&name=Crude%20Oil%20WTI [Accessed 22 Jan. 2015].

Pesek, W. (2015). *Japan's Hope May Be Its Hinterlands*. [online] BloombergView.com. Available at: http://www.bloombergview.com/articles/2015-01-27/bank-of-japan-must-get-creative-with-quantitative-easing-program [Accessed 18 Jan. 2015].

Sieg, L. (2015). *Japan's 'Abenomics' feared in trouble as challenges build*. [online] Reuters. Available at: http://www.reuters.com/article/2014/09/02/us-japan-economy-abenomics-idUSKBN0GX0VY20140902 [Accessed 5 Jan. 2015].

The Economist, (2014). Japan's Quantitative Easing; A Bigger Bazooka.

Thomas, L. (2006). *Money, Banking and Financial Markets*. Ohio: Thomas Learning. Inc., p.598.

Vickery, W. (1993). Full Employment Definition. [online] Available at: http://bilbo.economicoutlook.net/blog/?p=22154 [Accessed 21 Dec. 2014].

Weidmann, J. (2014). *Reforms for Recovery and Resilience*.

Wolf, M. (2014). *The Shifts and The Shocks*. Milton Keynes: Penguin, p.356

<u>**Appendices**</u>

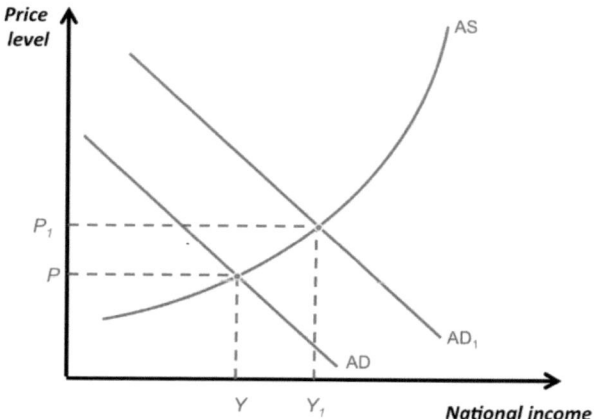

Figure 1.1: Revision Guru (2015). *Aggregate Demand*. Available:
http://revisionguru.co.uk/revisionguru/wp-content/uploads/2013/01/Slide041-
1024x767.jpg. Last accessed 29th December 2014.

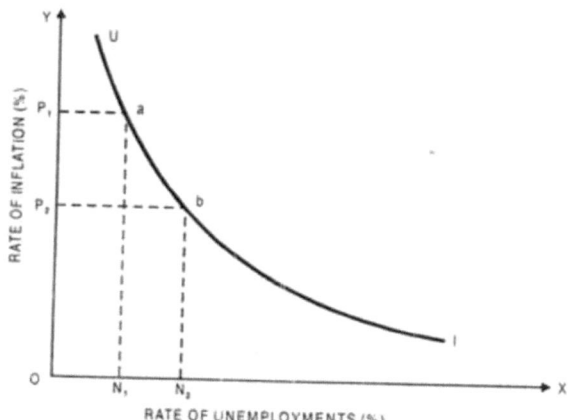

Fig. 3 The Phillips Curve: Unemployment-Inflation trade-off

Figure 1.2: Chand, S. (2014). *Conflict Between Objectives of Full Employment and Price
Stabilisation.* Available: http://cdn.yourarticlelibrary.com/wp-content/uploads/2014/02/
clip_image002_thumb2_thumb1.jpg. Last accessed 15th Dec 2014.

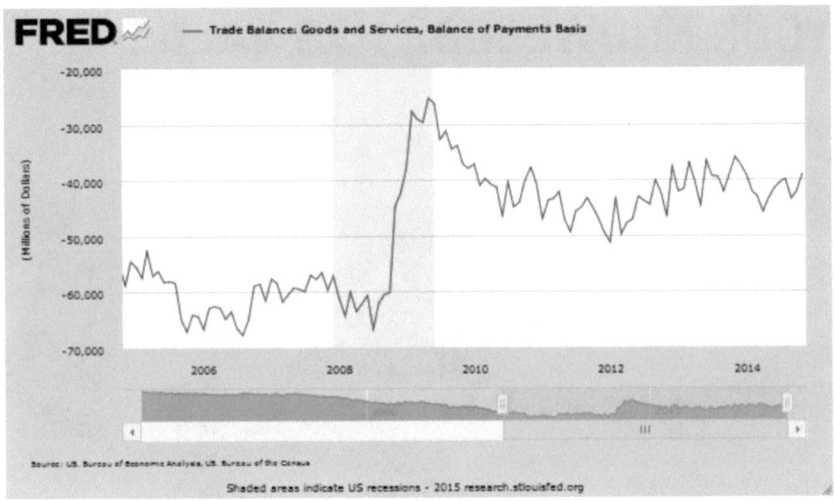

Figure 1.3: Federal Bank of St. Louis. (2015). *Graph: Trade Balance: Goods and Services, Balance of Payments Basis.* Available: http://research.stlouisfed.org/fred2/graph/?g=mK1. Last accessed 22nd January 2014.